066 BEHIND THE WALL: IT'S NOT OVER FOR WOMEN

By

Michael W. Couch

D.MIN, Pastor of Berean Baptist Church in Philadelphia, PA

Copyright Michael W. Couch

All rights reserved. No part of this book may be used or reproduced by any means, graphic, electronic, or mechanical, including photocopying, recording, taping, or by any information storage retrieval system, without the written permission of the publisher except in the case of brief quotations embodied in critical articles and reviews.

CONTENTS

Summary 1

Embracing Your Second Chance 5

Walking Through the Valley 9

God Hears Your Call 13

Strength for Your Second Chance 17

Overcoming Through Christ 21

Pressed But Not Crushed 25

God Is Within You 29

Trusting God's Plan 33

God's Plans for You 37

Hunger for Righteousness 41

Blessed Belief 45

All Things Work Together for Good 49

Shifting Your Mindset 53

Strength Through Christ 57

Summary

M.W. Couch, D.MIN, the dedicated pastor of Berean Baptist Church in Philadelphia, PA, brings a raw and real message to those incarcerated in his book, "066 Behind The Wall: It's Not Over." Written in an urban voice that resonates deeply with the reader, Couch's words offer a beacon of hope, faith, and the assurance that life's chapters continue beyond the prison walls.

Introduction:

In the introduction, Pastor Couch sets the stage by addressing the reality of life behind bars. He speaks directly to the hearts of those feeling lost, abandoned, and hopeless, reminding them that their current situation is not the end. God has a purpose for everyone, and it's never too late to start anew.

Chapter 1: Finding Hope in the Darkness

Drawing inspiration from Deuteronomy 31:8, Couch emphasizes that God is always present, even in the darkest times. He reassures readers that God has already gone before them, preparing a way out of their struggles. This chapter encourages finding hope and strength in God's unwavering presence.

Chapter 2: Walking Through the Valley

Using Psalm 23:4, Couch discusses the importance of courage and faith when navigating life's darkest valleys. He illustrates that, with God's guidance, one can face fears and emerge stronger. This chapter is a call to embrace the journey with trust in God's protective presence.

Chapter 3: God Hears Your Cry

Focusing on Psalm 145:18, Couch reassures that God is near to all who call on Him in truth. He encourages honest and heartfelt prayers, sharing personal stories and testimonies that demonstrate God's responsiveness and love. This chapter is about connecting deeply with God through prayer.

Chapter 4: Strength in the Struggle

Isaiah 41:10 serves as the foundation here, where Couch talks about finding strength in God during tough times. He highlights God's promise to uphold His people, offering practical advice on relying on God's strength to overcome challenges.

Chapter 5: Overcoming the World

In this chapter, based on John 16:33, Couch reminds readers that Jesus has already overcome the world's troubles. He encourages a mindset of victory, inspiring readers to face life's challenges with confidence in Christ's triumph.

Chapter 6: Pressed But Not Crushed

Using 2 Corinthians 4:8-9, Couch discusses resilience and the ability to withstand life's pressures. He emphasizes that while life may press hard, it will not crush those who rely on God. This chapter provides practical advice on maintaining faith and hope amidst trials.

Chapter 7: Trusting God's Plan

With Jeremiah 29:11, Couch reassures that God's plans are for good, to give hope and a future. He encourages trust in God's perfect plan and the belief that better days are ahead, regardless of past mistakes.

Shifting Your Mindset

In this chapter, Couch explores Philippians 4:8, stressing the power of positive thinking and focusing on what is true and noble. He teaches how aligning thoughts with God's truth can transform one's life.

Strength Through Christ

Philippians 4:13 is the focus here, where Couch empowers readers to find their strength in Christ. He reassures that through Christ, all things are possible, inspiring readers to pursue their dreams with confidence and faith.

Believing in God's Promises

Using Luke 1:45, Couch emphasizes the blessings that come from believing in God's promises. He encourages readers to hold on to their faith and trust that God's word will be fulfilled in their lives.

Conclusion: Embracing Your Second Chance

The conclusion ties all the messages together, reinforcing that it's not over. Couch encourages readers to embrace their second chance, trust in God's promises, and walk boldly into the future God has prepared for them. He leaves them with a powerful reminder that their story is still being written and that with God, their best days are ahead.

Embracing Your Second Chance

Scripture: Deuteronomy 31:8 - "The LORD himself goes before you and will be with you; he will never leave you nor forsake you. Do not be afraid; do not be discouraged."

Introduction:

Good evening, family. Today, we're diving into a powerful message from Deuteronomy 31:8, a message of hope and encouragement for all of us, especially those who've faced the challenges of incarceration. Life has a way of throwing us into dark places, but let me tell you, it's not over. Your story is far from finished.

1. God Goes Before You:

The Lord Himself goes before you. Understand this, before you even walked out of those prison gates, God was already making a way. He's been preparing your path, setting you up for a comeback. The mistakes of your past do not define your future. God is the author of your story, and He's writing a new chapter for you.

2. God Is With You:

You might feel alone in this new journey, but remember, God is with you. When friends turn their backs and society judges, God stands by your side. He sees your potential, your worth, and your dreams. He will never leave you nor forsake you. In every step you take, He's right there with you, guiding and protecting you.

3. Do Not Be Afraid:

Fear is a powerful enemy, but our God is more powerful. You've faced the darkness of incarceration; now it's time to step into the light without fear. The road ahead might be tough, filled with obstacles and doubters, but fear has no place in your heart. With God on your side, you can overcome anything.

4. Do Not Be Discouraged:

Discouragement is real, especially when you're trying to rebuild. But let this scripture remind you, do not be discouraged. Every setback is a setup for a comeback. Each failure is a stepping stone towards your success. Keep your head up, stay focused on God's promises, and push through the trials.

5. Embrace Your Second Chance:

This is your second chance, a new beginning. Embrace it with both hands. Remember Joseph from the Bible? Sold into slavery, thrown into prison, but God had a plan. Joseph's story didn't end in the pit or the prison. He rose to a place of power because he trusted God's plan. Your journey might be similar. Trust that God has a plan for you, a plan to prosper you and not to harm you, to give you hope and a future (Jeremiah 29:11).

Conclusion:

Family, let's walk out of here today with our heads held high, knowing that it's not over. Your past is behind you, and a bright future awaits. Deuteronomy 31:8 reminds us that God is with us, He goes before us, and He will never forsake us. So, don't be afraid and don't be discouraged. Embrace your second chance with faith and determination. God's got you, and your best days are ahead.

Let's pray. Prayer:

Heavenly Father, we thank You for Your unwavering presence in our lives. We thank You for going before us and making a way. Lord, I lift up everyone here today, especially those affected by incarceration. Remind them that their past does not define them and that You have a plan for their lives. Give them strength to face their fears and courage to overcome discouragement.

May they embrace their second chance with confidence, knowing that You are with them every step of the way. In Jesus' name, we pray.

Amen.

Go forth and live in the power of your second chance! It's not over!

Walking Through the Valley

Scripture: Psalm 23:4 - "Even though I walk through the darkest valley, I will fear no evil, for you are with me; your rod and your staff, they comfort me."

Introduction:

Good evening, family. Today, we gather to find strength and hope in the Word of God. We're focusing on Psalm 23:4, a verse that speaks directly to those who've walked through the darkest valleys. For our brothers and sisters affected by incarceration, hear me when I say: it's not over. Your journey is just beginning.

1. Walking Through the Darkest Valley:

Let's be real—life can hit hard. Being incarcerated is like walking through a dark valley. It's a place where hope feels distant, and fear looms large. But listen to the Psalmist: "Even though I walk through the darkest valley." Notice it says "walk through," not "stay in." This valley isn't your final destination; it's a part of your journey.

2. Fear No Evil:

Fear is real, especially when you're stepping back into the world. Fear of judgment, fear of failure, fear of the unknown. But the Psalmist says, "I will fear no evil." Why? Because God is with you. He's your protector and your guide. No matter what shadows lurk in the valley, remember that God's light shines brighter.

3. God Is With You:

"For you are with me." These words are a promise. Even in the darkest places, God has not abandoned you. When you were behind bars, He was there. As you step into your new life, He is with you. You are never alone. His presence is your constant companion, your source of strength, and your reason to hope.

4. The Rod and Staff:

"Your rod and your staff, they comfort me." God's rod and staff symbolize His guidance and protection. The rod is for defending you against the enemy, and the staff is for guiding you back when you stray. Trust in His tools of love and discipline. They are there to keep you safe and on the right path.

5. Embracing Your Second Chance:

This is your second chance, your opportunity to write a new chapter. Your past does not define your future. Think about David, who wrote this Psalm. He had his own share of dark valleys, yet he rose to be a king. Your journey might have been tough, but God is preparing you for something greater. Embrace your second chance with faith and determination.

Conclusion:

Family, remember Psalm 23:4 as you move forward. Your valley is not the end—it's just a part of your journey. Fear no evil because God is with you. His rod and staff are there to guide and protect you. It's not over; in fact, it's just beginning. Walk with confidence, knowing that God's got you and your best days are still ahead.

Let's pray. Prayer:

Heavenly Father, we come before You, grateful for Your unwavering presence in our lives. We thank You for walking with us through our darkest valleys and for Your promise of comfort and protection. Lord, I lift up every person here today, especially those affected by incarceration. Remind them that their past does not define them and that You have a glorious plan for their future. Give them the courage to face their fears and the strength to embrace their second chance. May they walk in the light of Your love, knowing that You are with them every step of the way. In Jesus' name, we pray.

Amen.

Go forth with the assurance that it's not over. Walk through your valley with faith and determination, for God is with you!

God Hears Your Call

Scripture: Psalm 145:18 - "The Lord is near to all who call on him, to all who call on him in truth."

Introduction:

Good evening, family. Today, we are here to find hope and encouragement in the Word of God. Our focus is on Psalm 145:18, a powerful reminder that no matter where we've been or what we've done, God is always near to us. For those who've been affected by incarceration, listen closely: it's not over. Your cries are heard, and your second chance is at hand.

1. The Lord is Near:

Let's start with the basics: "The Lord is near to all who call on him." This means that no matter how far you feel from grace, God is right there. He hasn't abandoned you. Even in the darkest cells and the loneliest moments, God was with you, and He's still with you now. His presence is constant, unyielding, and full of love.

2. Call on Him:

Calling on God isn't just about saying words; it's about reaching out with your heart. When you call on Him in truth, you're opening yourself up to His grace and mercy. Your past mistakes, your regrets, and your pain are all laid bare before Him. But remember, God's love is bigger than your past. He's ready to listen, to comfort, and to guide you.

3. In Truth:

To call on God in truth means to be real with Him. Drop the masks, the pretense, and the shame. God knows your story, every single chapter. He's not shocked by your failures; He's ready to rewrite your future. Honesty with God leads to healing. It's in those moments of raw truth that He begins to work wonders in your life.

4. Your Second Chance:

God specializes in second chances. Look at the story of Paul in the Bible. Once a persecutor of Christians, he had a radical encounter with Jesus and became one of the most influential apostles. Your story can have that same transformation. Your incarceration is a part of your past, but it doesn't define your future. God is giving you a second chance to rise, to rebuild, and to be a beacon of hope to others.

5. Embrace the Journey:

The road ahead might be challenging, but don't be discouraged. Psalm 145:18 assures us that God is near to those who call on Him. Lean into that promise. Embrace your journey with faith, knowing that God walks with you every step of the way. He hears your prayers, He sees your struggles, and He's paving a way for your comeback.

Conclusion:

Family, take Psalm 145:18 to heart. Know that "The Lord is near to all who call on him, to all who call on him in truth." Your cries for help, your prayers for a better tomorrow—they are all heard by God. It's not over; in fact, it's just the beginning. Your second chance is here. Embrace it with faith and courage, for God is with you, and He's ready to transform your life.

Let's pray. Prayer:

Heavenly Father, we come before You with hearts full of hope and gratitude. Thank You for being near to us, for hearing our cries, and for offering us a second chance. Lord, I lift up every person here today, especially those affected by incarceration. Remind them that their past does not dictate their future and that You have a plan for their lives. Give them the strength to call on You in truth, to be honest and open, and to embrace the new path You've set before them. May they walk with confidence, knowing that You are near, guiding and loving them every step of the way. In Jesus' name, we pray.

Amen.

Remember, family, it's not over. God hears your call, and your second chance is now. Walk in His love and grace, and watch as He transforms your life.

Strength for Your Second Chance

Scripture: Isaiah 41:10 - "So do not fear, for I am with you; do not be dismayed, for I am your God. I will strengthen you and help you; I will uphold you with my righteous right hand."

Introduction:

Good evening, family. Today, we come together to find strength and encouragement in the Word of God. Our focus is on Isaiah 41:10, a powerful promise from God to His people. For those who've been affected by incarceration, this message is for you: it's not over. God is with you, and He's offering you strength for your second chance.

1. Do Not Fear:

Life can be overwhelming, especially when you're trying to rebuild after incarceration. Fear of the unknown, fear of rejection, and fear of failure can paralyze you. But God says, "Do not fear, for I am with you." Fear has no place in your heart when you know that the Creator of the universe is walking with you. His presence is your courage.

2. Do Not Be Dismayed:

It's easy to feel dismayed when you look at the challenges ahead. But God reassures us, "Do not be dismayed, for I am your God." Remember who your God is. He is the Almighty, the all-powerful, and He's got your back. No matter how tough the road ahead seems, He's got a plan and a purpose for you.

3. God's Strength and Help:

"I will strengthen you and help you." This is God's promise. Your strength might fail, but God's strength is limitless. When you're weak, He is strong. When you're overwhelmed, He offers help. You don't have to do this alone. Lean on Him, and let His strength fill you up. He will help you overcome every obstacle.

4. Upheld by God's Righteous Right Hand:

God promises to uphold you with His righteous right hand. This means He will support you, lift you, and keep you steady. Think about that: the same hand that created the heavens and the earth is holding you up. You're not just anyone—you're a child of God, and He's committed to seeing you through.

5. Embrace Your Second Chance:

Your past is not your future. Just like Peter, who denied Jesus three times yet was restored and became a pillar of the early church, you too can rise from your past. Your second chance is here. Embrace it with faith. God's promise in Isaiah 41:10 is your assurance that you can move forward without fear or dismay, relying on His strength and support.

Conclusion:

Family, take Isaiah 41:10 to heart. "So do not fear, for I am with you; do not be dismayed, for I am your God. I will strengthen you and help you; I will uphold you with my righteous right hand."

Your journey isn't over. God is with you, ready to strengthen and help you. Your second chance is here. Walk in faith, knowing that God's righteous right hand is upholding you every step of the way.

Let's pray. Prayer:

Heavenly Father, we thank You for Your powerful promise in Isaiah 41:10. Thank You for being with us, for calming our fears, and for giving us strength. Lord, I lift up everyone here today, especially those affected by incarceration. Remind them that their past does not define their future and that You are their strength and support. Help them to embrace their second chance with confidence, knowing that

You are upholding them with Your righteous right hand. In Jesus' name, we pray.

Amen.

Remember, family, it's not over. God is with you, strengthening and helping you. Embrace your second chance and walk in the assurance of His love and support.

Overcoming Through Christ

Scripture: John 16:33 - "I have told you these things, so that in me you may have peace. In this world you will have trouble. But take heart! I have overcome the world."

Introduction:

Good evening, family. Today, we're diving into a message of hope and victory from John 16:33. This verse speaks directly to those of us who have faced the harsh realities of life, especially those affected by incarceration. Hear me clearly: it's not over. Jesus has overcome the world, and through Him, you can too.

1. Acknowledge the Trouble:

"In this world, you will have trouble." Let's be real—life is tough. You've faced challenges, setbacks, and disappointments. Incarceration has been a part of your journey, and it brought its own set of troubles. But Jesus doesn't sugarcoat it. He acknowledges that trouble is a part of life. The important thing is to recognize that trouble doesn't define you; how you respond to it does.

2. Finding Peace in Jesus:

Jesus says, "I have told you these things, so that in me you may have peace." Peace isn't about the absence of trouble; it's about finding calm in the midst of chaos. Jesus offers a peace that the world can't give. This peace comes from knowing that no matter what you've been through, Jesus is with you. He's got your back. When you lean into Him, you find a peace that surpasses all understanding.

3. Take Heart:

"But take heart!" These three words are a call to courage. Life after incarceration can be daunting. You might feel the weight of judgment, the fear of failure, or the uncertainty of the future. But Jesus calls you to take heart, to be courageous, because He has a plan for you. Courage isn't the absence of fear; it's moving forward in spite of it, knowing that Jesus walks with you.

4. Jesus Has Overcome:

"I have overcome the world." This is the cornerstone of our faith. Jesus faced the ultimate trouble—He was crucified, but He rose again, defeating sin and death. His victory is our victory. No matter how dark your past, no matter the struggles you face now, Jesus has already won the battle. Through Him, you can overcome any obstacle.

5. Embracing Your Second Chance:

Your past is part of your story, but it's not the end. Just like Paul, who went from persecuting Christians to becoming one of the greatest apostles, you too have a future filled with purpose and promise. Jesus offers you a second chance. Embrace it. Use your experiences to grow, to inspire, and to help others. Your testimony can be a beacon of hope to those who are walking through their own troubles.

Conclusion:

Family, hold onto John 16:33: "I have told you these things, so that in me you may have peace. In this world you will have trouble. But take heart! I have overcome the world." Remember, it's not over. Jesus has already secured your victory. Walk in His peace, take heart, and embrace your second chance with courage and faith.

Let's pray. Prayer:

Heavenly Father, we thank You for the powerful promise in John 16:33. Thank You for the peace that Jesus offers and for His victory over the world. Lord, I lift up everyone here today, especially those affected by incarceration. Remind them that their past does not define their future and that through Jesus, they can overcome any obstacle. Give them the courage to take heart and embrace their second chance.

Fill them with Your peace and guide them on their journey. In Jesus' name, we pray.

Amen.

Family, remember, it's not over. Through Christ, you have the power to overcome. Walk in His peace and victory, and watch as He transforms your life.

Pressed But Not Crushed

Scripture: 2 Corinthians 4:8-9 - "We are hard pressed on every side, but not crushed; perplexed, but not in despair; persecuted, but not abandoned; struck down, but not destroyed."

Introduction:

Good evening, family. Today, we're diving into a powerful message of resilience and hope from 2 Corinthians 4:8-9. This scripture speaks directly to the heart of those who've faced hard times, especially those affected by incarceration. Listen closely: it's not over. Your story is still being written, and through God's strength, you can rise again.

1. Pressed But Not Crushed:

"We are hard pressed on every side, but not crushed." Life's pressures can feel overwhelming, like the weight of the world is on your shoulders. Incarceration brings its own kind of pressure—separation from loved ones, the stigma, the struggle to rebuild. But hear this: being pressed doesn't mean you're crushed. You're stronger than you think, and God's strength in you is greater than any pressure from the world.

2. Perplexed But Not in Despair:

"Perplexed, but not in despair." There are times when you might not understand why things happen the way they do. You might feel confused and lost, wondering how to move forward. But remember, confusion doesn't lead to despair. When you put your trust in God, He gives clarity in the chaos and hope in the confusion. He's got a plan, even when you can't see it yet.

3. Persecuted But Not Abandoned:

"Persecuted, but not abandoned." You may have faced judgment, rejection, and persecution from people around you. Society can be harsh, and the label of incarceration can stick. But let me remind you, you are never abandoned. God is with you, always. He sees you, He knows your worth, and He will never leave you. When the world turns its back, God opens His arms.

4. Struck Down But Not Destroyed:

"Struck down, but not destroyed." Life has knocked you down, no doubt about it. You've faced some hard hits. But being knocked down isn't the end. You're still here, still standing. God's promise is that no matter how many times you're struck down, you will not be destroyed. His power in you is greater than any force against you.

5. Embrace Your Second Chance:

Your past is part of your journey, but it doesn't define your destination. Think about Peter, who denied Jesus three times but was restored and became a pillar of the early church. Your second chance is here, right now. Embrace it. Use your experiences as fuel to propel you forward, to inspire others, and to build a future rooted in faith and resilience.

Conclusion:

Family, hold onto 2 Corinthians 4:8-9: "We are hard pressed on every side, but not crushed; perplexed, but not in despair; persecuted, but not abandoned; struck down, but not destroyed." Remember, it's not over. Through God's strength, you can rise from any setback. Walk with your head held high, knowing that God's power is at work in you and your best days are ahead.

Let's pray. Prayer:

Heavenly Father, we thank You for the powerful promise in 2 Corinthians 4:8-9. Thank You for being our strength when we are pressed, our hope when we are perplexed, our constant companion when we are persecuted, and our resilience when we are struck down. Lord, I lift up everyone here today, especially those affected by incarceration. Remind them that their past does not define their future and that through You, they can overcome any obstacle. Give them the courage to embrace their second chance and walk in Your power. In Jesus' name, we pray.

Amen.

Family, remember, it's not over. God's strength is your strength. Embrace your second chance and walk boldly into the future He has for you.

God Is Within You

Scripture: Psalm 46:5 - "God is within her, she will not fall; God will help her at break of day."

Introduction:

Good evening, sisters. Today, we're focusing on a powerful message from Psalm 46:5. This verse is a reminder that no matter where you are, no matter what you've been through, God is within you. It's not over. Your strength, your hope, and your future are all secured by God's presence in your life.

1. God Is Within Her:

"God is within her..." This is a powerful statement. It means that God's presence is not just around you but within you. His spirit, His strength, and His love are part of who you are. Being in prison might make you feel separated from everything you once knew, but remember, nothing can separate you from God's presence. He's with you right here, right now.

Illustration:

Think about a lighthouse in the middle of a storm. The waves crash against it, the wind howls, but the light inside remains steady and strong. You are like that lighthouse. The storms of life might rage around you, but God's presence within you keeps your light shining. It's not over. Your inner light, fueled by God's spirit, will guide you through the darkest nights.

2. She Will Not Fall:

"...she will not fall..." With God within you, you have a foundation that cannot be shaken. Life's challenges, mistakes, and regrets might try to knock you down, but you will not fall. God's strength upholds you. This doesn't mean you won't face hard times; it means those hard times won't defeat you. You are stronger than you think because God is your strength.

3. God Will Help Her at Break of Day:

"God will help her at break of day." This is a promise of God's timely intervention. No matter how dark the night, the dawn is coming. God's help is on the way. He sees your struggles, hears your prayers, and He's working on your behalf. Trust that your breakthrough is coming. Morning always follows the darkest part of the night.

4. Embrace Your Second Chance:

Your current situation is not your final destination. Look at Ruth in the Bible, who lost everything but found redemption and a new beginning. Or the woman at the well, who met Jesus and had her life transformed. Your story isn't over. God specializes in turning messes into messages and tests into testimonies. Embrace this second chance with faith, knowing that God is writing a new chapter for you.

Illustration:

Consider a caterpillar in a cocoon. It seems like the end, confined and restricted. But inside that cocoon, a transformation is happening. When it's ready, it emerges as a beautiful butterfly. You might feel confined and restricted right now, but God is transforming you from the inside out. It's not over. Your wings are coming, and you will soar.

Conclusion:

Sisters, hold Psalm 46:5 close to your heart: "God is within her, she will not fall; God will help her at break of day." Remember, it's not over. God is within you, giving you strength and hope. He will help you, and your breakthrough is coming. Trust in His presence, embrace your second chance, and watch as God transforms your life.

Let's pray. Prayer:

Heavenly Father, we thank You for Your powerful presence within us. Thank You for being our strength and our hope. Lord, I lift up every woman here today. You know their struggles, their fears, and their dreams. Fill them with Your spirit, remind them that they will not fall, and help them to trust in Your promise of a new day. Embrace them with Your love and guide them through this journey. In Jesus' name, we pray.

Amen.

Remember, sisters, it's not over. God is within you, and He's guiding you to a new beginning. Stay strong, keep the faith, and know that your best days are ahead.

Trusting God's Plan

Scripture: Proverbs 3:5-6 - "Trust in the Lord with all your heart and lean not on your own understanding; in all your ways submit to him, and he will make your paths straight."

Introduction:

Good evening, sisters. Today, we're diving into a powerful message from Proverbs 3:5-6. This verse is all about trust—trusting in God's plan, even when life doesn't make sense. For those of us behind the wall, this message is crucial. It's not over. God's plan for you is still unfolding, and when you trust Him, He will guide you to a brighter future.

1. Trust in the Lord with All Your Heart:

"Trust in the Lord with all your heart." Trust isn't always easy, especially when life feels like it's falling apart. But trusting God means believing that He's got your back, even when things look bleak. It means putting your whole heart into believing that God's got a plan for you, one that's good and full of hope.

Illustration:

Think about a GPS. When you're driving, and you don't know the way, you trust the GPS to guide you. Sometimes, it takes you on routes that don't make sense, but you follow it because you trust it knows the way. God's guidance is like that GPS. You might not always understand the route He's taking you on, but trust that He knows the way to your destination. It's not over. God is leading you to a place of hope and restoration.

2. Lean Not on Your Own Understanding:

"...and lean not on your own understanding." Our own understanding is limited. We see only a part of the picture, but God sees it all. Leaning on your own understanding can lead to confusion, frustration, and despair. Instead, lean on God. Trust that He knows what He's doing, even when you don't.

3. In All Your Ways Submit to Him:

"In all your ways, submit to him." Submission to God means surrendering your plans, your fears, and your doubts to Him. It means saying, "God, I don't have all the answers, but I trust that You do." It's about letting go and letting God take control. When you submit to Him, you open the door for His blessings and guidance.

4. He Will Make Your Paths Straight:

"...and he will make your paths straight." This is a promise. When you trust in God and submit to His will, He will direct your path. He will take the crooked, broken roads and make them straight. Your past doesn't define your future. God is in the business of making new paths, opening new doors, and creating new opportunities.

Illustration:

Consider a mosaic. It's made up of broken pieces of glass and pottery, but when the artist puts it together, it becomes a beautiful piece of art. Your life might feel like a bunch of broken pieces right now, but God is the master artist. He's taking those broken pieces and creating something beautiful. It's not over. Your life is becoming a masterpiece in His hands.

Conclusion:

Sisters, hold Proverbs 3:5-6 close to your heart: "Trust in the Lord with all your heart and lean not on your own understanding; in all your ways submit to him, and he will make your paths straight." Remember, it's not over. Trust in God, submit to His will and watch as He makes your paths straight. He's guiding you to a future full of hope and promise.

Let's pray. Prayer:

Heavenly Father, we thank You for Your promise to guide us when we trust in You. Thank You for making our paths straight, even when we don't understand the way. Lord, I lift up every woman here today. You know their struggles, their fears, and their hopes. Help them to trust in You with all their hearts, to lean on Your understanding, and to submit to Your will. Remind them that it's not over and that You are creating a beautiful future for them. In Jesus' name, we pray.

Amen.

Remember, sisters, it's not over. Trust in God's plan, lean on His understanding and let Him guide you to a new and brighter future. Your best days are ahead.

God's Plans for You

Scripture: Jeremiah 29:11 - "For I know the plans I have for you," declares the Lord, "plans to prosper you and not to harm you, plans to give you hope and a future."

Introduction:

Good evening, sisters. Today, we're diving into a powerful promise from Jeremiah 29:11. This verse is a reminder that no matter where you are, no matter what you've been through, God has a plan for your life. It's not over. Your journey is just beginning, and God's plans for you are full of hope and a bright future.

1. God Knows the Plans He Has for You:

"For I know the plans I have for you," declares the Lord..." God's plans for you are not random; they are intentional and personal. He knows every detail of your life and has crafted a plan specifically for you. Even behind these walls, His plans are at work. You are not forgotten, and your life has purpose.

Illustration:

Think about an architect designing a building. The architect has a detailed plan, knowing exactly how the building will look and function. Right now, you might feel like a construction site, messy and incomplete. But God, the ultimate architect, has a detailed plan for your life. He sees the finished masterpiece, even when you can't. It's not over. Your life is a work in progress, and God's plan is unfolding beautifully.

2. Plans to Prosper You and Not to Harm You:

"...plans to prosper you and not to harm you..." God's intentions for you are good. He wants to see you thrive, to live a life full of joy and purpose. Being in prison might make you feel like prosperity is out of reach, but God's definition of prosperity goes beyond material wealth. It's about spiritual growth, inner peace, and a sense of fulfillment that comes from knowing Him.

3. Plans to Give You Hope and a Future:

"...plans to give you hope and a future." Hope is a powerful thing. It's the light in the darkness, the belief that tomorrow can be better than today. God's plans for you include a future filled with hope. No matter how bleak things look right now, God's promise stands. He has a future for you that's full of possibilities.

4. Embrace Your Second Chance:

Your current situation does not define your entire story. Look at Joseph in the Bible, who was sold into slavery and later imprisoned, yet he rose to become a powerful leader in Egypt. Or think of Rahab, who went from a life of shame to being part of the lineage of Jesus. Your past doesn't disqualify you from God's future for you. Embrace this second chance with faith, knowing that God's plans are still in motion.

Illustration:

Imagine a potter working with clay. The clay starts out as a lump, with no shape or purpose. But in the hands of the potter, it's molded and shaped into something beautiful and useful. Right now, you might feel like that lump of clay, but God, the master potter, is shaping you into something extraordinary. It's not over. Your transformation is underway, and your future is in God's hands.

Conclusion:

Sisters, hold Jeremiah 29:11 close to your heart: "For I know the plans I have for you," declares the Lord, "plans to prosper you and not to harm you, plans to give you hope and a future." Remember, it's not over. Trust in God's plans, embrace your second chance, and watch as He leads you to a future full of hope and purpose.

Let's pray. Prayer:

Heavenly Father, we thank You for Your promises and the plans You have for us. Thank You for seeing our potential and our future, even when we can't. Lord, I lift up every woman here today. You know their struggles, their fears, and their dreams. Fill them with hope, remind them of Your plans for their lives, and give them the strength to embrace their second chance. Let them feel Your love and guidance as they move forward. In Jesus' name, we pray.

Amen.

Remember, sisters, it's not over. Trust in God's plans for you, embrace your future with hope, and know that your best days are ahead. God's got you, and He's leading you to a life full of purpose and promise.

Hunger for Righteousness

Scripture: Matthew 5:6 - "Blessed are those who hunger and thirst for righteousness, for they will be filled."

Introduction:

Good evening, sisters. Today, we're diving into a powerful message from Matthew 5:6. This verse is all about a deep desire for righteousness—a hunger and thirst that God promises to satisfy. Even behind these walls, your journey is far from over. God sees your desire for a new life, and He's ready to fill you with His righteousness and blessings.

1. Blessed Are Those Who Hunger and Thirst:

"Blessed are those who hunger and thirst for righteousness..." Hunger and thirst are strong desires. They represent a need that can't be ignored. When you hunger and thirst for righteousness, you're craving a life that's right with God. It's a deep, burning desire to live according to His will, to turn from past mistakes, and to embrace a new way of living.

Illustration:

Think about an athlete training for a big event. She's focused, dedicated, and pushing herself to the limit. She feels the hunger to win, the thirst for victory. Every drop of sweat, every muscle ache, brings her closer to her goal. In the same way, your hunger and thirst for righteousness is driving you towards a life that God has planned for you. It's not over. Your spiritual training is preparing you for a victory in Christ.

2. For Righteousness:

Righteousness isn't about being perfect; it's about striving to live in a way that honors God. It's about making choices that reflect His love, justice, and truth. Behind these walls, it might seem hard to live righteously but remember, it's about progress, not perfection. Each step you take towards God's way is a step in the right direction.

3. They Will Be Filled:

"...for they will be filled." This is a promise from God. When you hunger and thirst for righteousness, God will fill you. He won't leave you empty or wanting. He will satisfy your deepest needs and desires. He'll give you the strength to keep going, the peace to endure, and the joy to lift you up.

4. Embrace Your Second Chance:

Your past doesn't have to define your future. Look at the woman at the well in John 4. She had a past that she wasn't proud of, but Jesus offered her living water, a chance to start anew. She left her past behind and became a witness for Christ. Your story can have the same transformation. Embrace this second chance with a heart that hungers for God's righteousness.

Illustration:

Imagine a barren desert, dry and lifeless. Then picture rain pouring down, soaking into the ground, bringing new life. Flowers bloom, rivers flow, and the desert is transformed into a lush, vibrant place. Your soul might feel like that barren desert right now, but God's righteousness is the rain. It's not over. Let His love and truth soak into your life and bring forth new growth and beauty.

Conclusion:

Sisters, hold Matthew 5:6 close to your heart: "Blessed are those who hunger and thirst for righteousness, for they will be filled." Remember, it's not over. Your hunger and thirst for a better life, a righteous life, will be satisfied by God. He sees your desire for change and promises to fill you with His blessings. Keep striving, keep seeking, and watch how God transforms your life.

Let's pray. Prayer:

Heavenly Father, we thank You for Your promise to fill those who hunger and thirst for righteousness. Thank You for seeing our desires for a better life and for offering us Your righteousness. Lord, I lift up every woman here today. You know their struggles, their hopes, and their deepest desires. Fill them with Your Spirit, guide them on the path of righteousness, and remind them that it's not over. Let them feel Your love and peace as they embrace their second chance. In Jesus' name, we pray.

Amen.

Remember, sisters, it's not over. Your hunger and thirst for righteousness will be filled by God. Trust in His promises, embrace your second chance and watch as He fills your life with His love and blessings. Your best days are ahead.

Blessed Belief

Scripture: Luke 1:45 - "Blessed is she who has believed that the Lord would fulfill his promises to her!"

Introduction:

Good evening, sisters. Today, we're diving into a message of faith and fulfillment from Luke 1:45. This verse is about the power of believing in God's promises, even when it feels like all hope is lost. For those of us behind the wall, it's a reminder that it's not over. God's promises still stand, and our belief in them brings blessings beyond measure.

1. Blessed Is She Who Has Believed:

"Blessed is she who has believed..." Belief is a powerful thing. It's more than just thinking something might happen; it's trusting that it will. It's having faith that God's promises are true, even when our circumstances say otherwise. Being in prison might challenge your belief, but remember, your faith is the key to unlocking God's blessings.

Illustration:

Think about a gardener planting seeds. She can't see what's happening under the soil, but she believes that those seeds will sprout. She waters them, tends to them, and waits with hope.

Your faith is like those seeds. You might not see the growth yet, but believe that God is working beneath the surface. It's not over. Your belief is planting the seeds for a future harvest of blessings.

2. The Lord Would Fulfill His Promises:

"...that the Lord would fulfill his promises to her!" God's promises are rock solid. They're not dependent on our circumstances or our past mistakes. He promises hope, a future, and a new beginning. God's promises are for you, right where you are. He hasn't forgotten you, and He will fulfill what He has spoken over your life.

3. Embrace Your Second Chance:

Your current situation is not the end of your story. Look at Mary, the mother of Jesus. She believed God's promise to her, despite how impossible it seemed. She embraced her role in God's plan, and through her belief, the world was changed. Your belief in God's promises can also lead to incredible change, both in your life and in the lives of those around you.

Illustration:

Consider a butterfly struggling to emerge from its chrysalis. The process is difficult, but it's necessary for its wings to strengthen. Once free, the butterfly can soar. Your time behind these walls might feel like a struggle, but it's not over. God is strengthening you, preparing you to break free and soar into the destiny He has planned for you.

4. Hold on to Hope:

Believing in God's promises means holding on to hope, even when things seem bleak. It's about trusting that God's timing is perfect and that His plans for you are good. Hope is the anchor that keeps you steady through the storms, the light that guides you through the darkness.

Conclusion:

Sisters, take Luke 1:45 to heart: "Blessed is she who has believed that the Lord would fulfill his promises to her!" Remember, it's not over. Your belief in God's promises brings blessings that can transform your life. Keep the faith, embrace your second chance, and watch as God fulfills His promises to you.

Let's pray. Prayer:

Heavenly Father, we thank You for Your unwavering promises. Thank You for the blessings that come from believing in You. Lord, I lift up every woman here today. You know their struggles, their fears, and their hopes. Strengthen their faith, remind them of Your promises, and fill them with hope. Help them to believe that it's not over and that You are working in their lives. In Jesus' name, we pray.

Amen.

Remember, sisters, it's not over. Believe in God's promises, hold on to hope, and watch as He brings blessings into your life. Your best days are ahead, and God is with you every step of the way.

All Things Work Together for Good

Scripture: Romans 8:28 - "And we know that in all things God works for the good of those who love him, who have been called according to his purpose."

Introduction:

Good evening, sisters. Today, we're diving into a powerful message from Romans 8:28. This verse is a beacon of hope and assurance that no matter where you are or what you've been through, God is working things out for your good. It's not over. God has a plan, and He's weaving everything together for your ultimate good and His glory.

1. All Things Work Together for Good:

"And we know that in all things God works for the good..." This is a promise from God. It doesn't say some things or most things—it says all things. That includes the good, the bad, and the ugly. Your experiences, your struggles, and even your mistakes are all part of God's plan to bring about good in your life.

Illustration:

Think about baking a cake. The individual ingredients like flour, raw eggs, and baking powder aren't very tasty on their own. But when you mix them together and bake them, they transform into something delicious. Your life might feel like a mix of unpleasant ingredients right now, but God is the master baker. He's mixing all those parts together and baking them into something beautiful and good. It's not over. God is creating something amazing out of your life.

2. For Those Who Love Him:

"...for the good of those who love him..." Loving God means trusting Him, even when life doesn't make sense. It means holding on to His promises, even when you can't see the way forward.

Your love for God aligns you with His purpose and opens the door for His blessings. He sees your heart and your desire to walk in His ways.

3. Called According to His Purpose:

"...who have been called according to his purpose." You have a purpose. God has called you, and He has a specific plan for your life. This calling isn't erased by your past or your mistakes. In fact, God can use your experiences to shape you and prepare you for the purpose He has set for you. Your journey is unique, and God's purpose for you is greater than any obstacle you face.

4. Embrace Your Second Chance:

Your current situation is not the end of your story. Look at Joseph in the Bible. He was sold into slavery, falsely accused, and thrown into prison. But God used all those experiences to prepare him for a position of great influence and to save many lives. Your past doesn't disqualify you from God's future for you. Embrace this second chance with faith, knowing that God is working everything together for your good.

Illustration:

Consider a tapestry. From the back, it looks like a mess of threads and knots. But when you turn it over, you see a beautiful picture. Right now, your life might look like that messy side of the tapestry, but God sees the other side. He's weaving a beautiful picture from your experiences.

It's not over. Trust that He's creating something beautiful in your life.

Conclusion:

Sisters, hold Romans 8:28 close to your heart: "And we know that in all things God works for the good of those who love him, who have been called according to his purpose."

Remember, it's not over. God is working everything together for your good. Trust in His plan, embrace your second chance, and watch as He transforms your life into something beautiful and purposeful.

Let's pray. Prayer:

Heavenly Father, we thank You for Your promise that all things work together for good for those who love You and are called according to Your purpose. Thank You for seeing beyond our past and working in our present to shape our future. Lord, I lift up every woman here today. You know their struggles, their fears, and their dreams. Fill them with hope, remind them that it's not over, and help them to trust in Your plan. In Jesus' name, we pray.

Amen.

Remember, sisters, it's not over. God is working all things together for your good. Trust in His purpose for you and embrace the beautiful future He has planned. Your best days are ahead, and God is with you every step of the way.

Shifting Your Mindset

Scripture: Philippians 4:8 - "Finally, brothers and sisters, whatever is true, whatever is noble, whatever is right, whatever is pure, whatever is lovely, whatever is admirable—if anything is excellent or praiseworthy—think about such things."

Introduction:

Good evening, sisters. Today, we're diving into a message from Philippians 4:8. This verse is about the power of our thoughts and how shifting our mindset can transform our lives. Even behind these walls, your story isn't over. God is calling you to focus on what's true and good, and in doing so, you can experience His peace and hope.

1. The Power of Thoughts:

"Finally, brothers and sisters, whatever is true, whatever is noble..." Our thoughts have incredible power. They shape our attitudes, our actions, and our outlook on life. When you're in a tough place, it's easy to let negative thoughts take over. But God calls us to focus on the positive, the true, and the good. This isn't just about positive thinking; it's about aligning our minds with God's truth.

Illustration:

Think of your mind like a garden. If you plant weeds and let them grow, they'll take over and choke out the good plants. But if you plant flowers and tend to them, your garden will flourish. Your thoughts are like those plants. Fill your mind with God's truth and goodness, and watch your life flourish. It's not over. Your garden can bloom beautifully, even here and now.

2. Whatever Is Noble and Right:

"...whatever is right, whatever is pure..." God's truth is noble and right. It's about focusing on what's honorable, what brings joy and peace. This might seem challenging in a place filled with negativity, but remember, your thoughts are under your control. Choose to dwell on what's right and pure, and you'll see a change in how you feel and live.

3. Whatever Is Lovely and Admirable:

"...whatever is lovely, whatever is admirable..." There is beauty in every situation, even in the hardest places. Look for what's lovely and admirable in your surroundings and in the people around you. It might be a kind word, a beautiful sunset, or an act of compassion. When you focus on these things, you open your heart to God's presence and peace.

4. If Anything Is Excellent or Praiseworthy:

"...if anything is excellent or praiseworthy—think about such things." God wants you to focus on excellence and praise. This doesn't mean ignoring the reality of your situation, but it means choosing to see the good and to praise God for His faithfulness. Your circumstances don't define your ability to worship and to find the excellent and praiseworthy in your life.

Illustration:

Imagine a radio station. You can choose which station to tune into. Some stations play negative, depressing music, while others play uplifting, joyful tunes. Your mind is like that radio. You have the power to tune into God's frequency, the one that plays His promises, His love, and His truth. It's not over. Tune into God's station, and let His music fill your life.

Conclusion:

Sisters, hold Philippians 4:8 close to your heart: "Finally, brothers and sisters, whatever is true, whatever is noble, whatever is right, whatever is pure, whatever is lovely, whatever is admirable—if anything is excellent or praiseworthy—think about such things." Remember, it's not over. Shift your mindset, focus on God's truth, and let His peace fill your life. You have the power to choose your thoughts, and in doing so, you can transform your experience, even behind these walls.

Let's pray. Prayer:

Heavenly Father, we thank You for the power of Your Word and the truth that it brings to our lives. Thank You for reminding us to focus on what is true, noble, right, pure, lovely, and admirable. Lord, I lift up every woman here today. You know their struggles, their fears, and their hopes. Help them to shift their mindset, to focus on Your truth, and to find peace and joy in Your presence. Remind them that it's not over, and that with You, their best days are ahead. In Jesus' name, we pray.

Amen.

Remember, sisters, it's not over. Choose to focus on what's true and good, and let God's peace transform your life. Your best days are ahead, and God is with you every step of the way.

Strength Through Christ

Scripture: Philippians 4:13 - "I can do all things through Christ who strengthens me."

Introduction:

Good evening, sisters. Today, we're diving into a powerful and uplifting message from Philippians 4:13. This verse is a declaration of strength and victory through Jesus Christ. No matter where you find yourself today, remember, it's not over. Through Christ, you have the strength to overcome any obstacle and achieve great things.

1. I Can Do All Things:

"I can do all things..." This is a bold statement. It means there are no limits to what you can achieve when you trust in Christ. It doesn't matter what your past looks like or the challenges you're facing now. God's power isn't limited by your circumstances. Believe that you can rise above your situation, achieve your dreams, and become the person God created you to be.

Illustration:

Think about a tree growing through concrete. It starts as a tiny seed, but it has the strength to break through the hard ground and reach for the sky. Your potential is like that seed. You might feel surrounded by concrete walls, but the strength Christ gives you can break through any barrier. It's not over. You have the power to grow and thrive, even in tough conditions.

2. Through Christ:

"...through Christ..." The source of your strength is not in your own abilities but in Christ. When you feel weak, He is your strength. When you feel lost, He is your guide. When you feel defeated, He is your victory. Lean on Him, and He will provide the power you need to overcome every challenge.

3. Who Strengthens Me:

"...who strengthens me." Jesus is the one who gives you the strength to keep going, to face each day with hope, and to overcome every obstacle. His strength is made perfect in your weakness. No matter how low you feel, His strength is available to lift you up and carry you through.

4. Embrace Your Second Chance:

Your current situation does not define your entire life. Look at Paul, who wrote these words while he was in prison. Despite his circumstances, he believed in the power of Christ to give him strength. Your story can have the same transformation. Embrace this second chance with faith, knowing that through Christ, you can do all things.

Illustration:

Consider a phoenix rising from the ashes. It's a symbol of rebirth and renewal. No matter how devastating the fire, the phoenix rises anew, stronger and more beautiful. You are like that phoenix. Through Christ, you have the strength to rise from the ashes of your past and embrace a new beginning. It's not over. Your story is one of strength, renewal, and victory.

Conclusion:

Sisters, hold Philippians 4:13 close to your heart: "I can do all things through Christ who strengthens me." Remember, it's not over. Through Christ, you have the strength to overcome every challenge, to rise above your circumstances, and to achieve your dreams. Lean on Him, trust in His power, and watch as He transforms your life.

Let's pray. Prayer:

Heavenly Father, we thank You for the strength that comes through Jesus Christ. Thank You for the promise that we can do all things through Him who strengthens us. Lord, I lift up every woman here today. You know their struggles, their fears, and their hopes. Fill them with Your strength, remind them that it's not over, and help them to trust in Your power. Guide them as they embrace their second chance and walk in Your victory. In Jesus' name, we pray.

Amen.

Remember, sisters, it's not over. Through Christ, you have the strength to face anything and to achieve great things. Your best days are ahead, and God is with you every step of the way.

Made in the USA
Middletown, DE
03 September 2024